27/2/06

R45726

Versace

FOR MY SECOND CHILD

THIS IS A CARLTON BOOK

Text and design copyright © 1999 Carlton Books Limited

This edition published by Carlton Books Limited 2000
20 Mortimer Street
London
W1N 7RD
www.carltonbooks.com

A CIP catalogue for this book is available from the British Library

ISBN 1 85868 880-9

Executive Editor: Sarah Larter
Art Director: Trevor Newman
Editor: Janice Anderson
Design: Simon Mercer
Picture research: Alex Pepper
Production: Garry Lewis

Printed and bound in Dubai

Versace

NICOLA WHITE

CARLTON

Perhaps the best-known fashion label

in the world, Versace is also one of the most lucrative. In autumn 1999, the ready-to-wear prices ranged from £80 for a pair of jeans, to £1,300 for a suit and £12,500 for a hand-beaded, floral appliqué two-piece. Despite Gianni Versace's notorious murder in Miami in July 1997, the company turnover reached almost £550 million in 1998.

This turnover is derived not only from the Versace group's fashion collections, but also from an extensive collection of accessories, fragrances and household products. Some of the products are made in the company factory, but most are manufactured under licence, in return for substantial royalties. The goods are sold in the 260 Versace boutiques around the world, and at over 3,000 sales points in department stores. It is not difficult to believe Gianni Versace's proclamation, published in *W* magazine in March 1992, that "I love money".

Because he made such good copy, much was and is still being written about Gianni Versace. He appeared almost daily in the world's press and was the subject of several glossy books, notably *Gianni Versace* and *Versace* by Richard Martin (both published in 1997). Attention was broadly divided between, on the one hand, books and magazines with a vested interest in Versace's continued success, which tended to offer unashamedly eulogistic accounts of his design skills and, on the other, the rather more critical attitude of newspaper journalists who were often most interested in digging the dirt on his private life, or his so-called "feud" with fellow Italian designer Giorgio Armani. This book attempts to steer a path between these two approaches, to offer a balanced appraisal of the Versace group and its work up to the end of the twentieth century, focusing on the reasons for its enormous success.

Gianni Versace has been variously portrayed by the media as "a talented vulgarian", " the supreme purveyor of flash trash", "the Prince of Glitz", "the Man with the Midas touch" and one who "turns women into whores and men into studs". These characterizations of his public persona certainly sum up a commonly held perception. Yet they conflict with the descriptions of Versace's personality by those who knew him: "a quiet gray-haired gentleman", according to *American Way* magazine, (1 August 1996); or this, in *The Guardian* newspaper, (16 July 1997): "very shy and very nice ... phenomenally generous and hospitable ... a charming man who not only remembered journalists' names but also those of their children or cats and never forgot to ask how they were ... he loved nothing more than settling down for the evening with his gardening and art books".

Versace, explained the enigma of his personality in the *American Way* article:

"I'M STILL THE LITTLE, PROVINCIAL shy boy WHO **FORCED HIMSELF** TO BE A public person.**"**

Gianni Versace's early years offer valuable insights into his subsequent approach to fashion. Born in Reggio di Calabria in 1946, Versace was fond of describing an idyllic childhood in southern Italy, with his brother Santo (born in 1944), his sister Donatella (born in 1956), and adoring, affluent parents. However, as the Channel 4 television documentary "Secret Lives", shown on 23 December 1997, revealed, Versace's perspective on his bourgeois childhood was a "reinvention"; he was, in fact, of fairly humble origins.

According to Nick Read, the director of the documentary, "His father, [Antonio], far from being a well-to-do businessman, ran a haberdashery and delivered butane gas" (*Sunday Times*, 14 December 1997). His mother Franca was a quality dressmaker who imported and copied (or "translated") French designs for a local conservative, middle-class clientele, as was typical in Italian fashion in those years. She had a small shop which sold buttons and accessories, in addition to garments. His parent's personalities also seem to have been romanticized. Versace's reputed first lover, Bruno de Robertis, a clothes designer who still lives in Calabria, recalled in "Secret Lives" that they both enjoyed inventing stories about their provenance, "only Gianni kept telling them after he left".

"The thing that made my life special," Versace told the *New Yorker* (28 July 1997) "was growing up in the south of Italy ... with a mother who was such a character, a father who was such a poet." Versace often spoke of his mother, who was clearly an important influence upon him: "the most important relationship was with my mother, who was a strong woman, ahead of her time ... a fascinating woman, very beautiful". He also said that he admired his father, but others remember him as a "cold and distant man who failed to protect his

VERSACE

effeminate son with a falsetto voice … from the mockery of bullies" in his home town (*Sunday Times* 14 December 1997).

Versace studied architecture between 1964 and 1967, but left college prematurely and started working with his mother as a designer and buyer. Soon, his mother's business began to attract a younger and more adventurous clientele, including Versace's first star client, the reigning Miss Italy, who offered him a valuable lesson in free publicity.

Central to the advancement of Versace's early career were the relationships he cultivated with representatives of the major Italian clothing manufacturers. His mentor was Gigi Monti, the founder of ready-to-wear label Basile, who designed for Missoni and Krizia and sold to Franca Versace's shop. Through Monti and other contacts, Versace began designing on a freelance basis for manufacturers in Tuscany and other areas of Italy.

Versace's timing was excellent. Italian fashion had been well-known on the international fashion stage since 1951, when the first collective international shows were staged in Florence. Although haute couture was the initial focus, Italy was especially admired for its easy-to-wear, elegant casuals which fitted exactly the postwar mood of its wealthy clientele, particularly in America. By the mid-1960s there was a clearly discernible, internationally-applauded Italian style in high-quality ready-to-wear. This style drew on the American tradition of casual sportswear, combined with native Italian traditions.

By the early 1970s, Milan, with its proximity to Italian textile production and clothing manufacture, was poised to become the centre of Italian high fashion ready-to-wear. Versace moved to Milan in 1972, to design ready-to-wear for Arnaldo Girombelli, one of the most important names in Italian fashion, and owner of the leading Callaghan, Genny and Complice labels. It was this move to Milan which reputedly caused a disagreement with his father which was not resolved until 1989.

By the late 1970s, there were a number of now-famous designers working in and around Milan, including Krizia, Armani and Ferré, as well as a group of quality ready-to-wear manufacturers, lead by MaxMara. Together they helped firmly to establish Milan as Italy's fashion capital and fostered Italy's burgeoning international fashion reputation.

One of the keys to the remarkable rise of Italian fashion has been the mutually beneficial relationship between fashion designers (and manufacturers) and textile companies. Versace enjoyed a close association with manufacturers of a full range of materials, including the silk company Ratti SpA, which produces the signature Versace prints. The group also developed strong links with clothing manufacturers, such as Ermenegildo Zegna, which produces Versace menswear.

IN 1978 VERSACE LAUNCHED HIS OWN **WOMENSWEAR LABEL** AND OPENED HIS FIRST BOUTIQUE, FOLLOWED IN 1979 BY HIS FIRST **MENSWEAR** COLLECTION. HE announced HIS FIRST COLLECTION TO THE WORLD IN THE AMERICAN HIGH-FASHION MAGAZINE **HARPER'S BAZAAR**, WITH AN ADVERTISEMENT WHICH READ "GIANNI VERSACE AND MILAN. HERE AND VERY NOW ... A TOTAL EXTRAVAGANCE. "

Within four years of his launch, Versace had won the prestigious Milanese Golden Eye award for his women's collection, and as such entered the top rank of international fashion designers.

Apart from the disagreement between Versace and his father, the family stuck together from the beginning, in typical Italian style. Donatella and Santo, in different ways, were unquestionably fundamental to the success of the label.

Santo, who remains the unsung hero of the organization, has always been responsible for the shrewd handling of the company's financial affairs. According to the late Sergio Galeotti, Giorgio Armani's business manager and companion, quoted in *The New Yorker* magazine (28 July 1977) "It was Santo who put them on a solid basis that allowed them to grow so fast. He found the investors ... the smartest thing they did was to invest in real estate in the centre of Milan before the prices took off ... it was brilliant financial strategy."

Following the death of their mother in 1978, Donatella became her brother's greatest creative influence, and from 1993, she became designer of the money-making diffusion labels Versus and Istante. Versace's long-term lover Antonio d'Amico co-ordinated the Versace Sport and Istante labels, and Donatella's husband, the American ex-model Paul Beck, is manager of the Versace company; alongside Donatella, he has always been closely involved with the advertising campaigns and image.

Amid all the hype that surrounds the Versace name, it is easy to forget that his clothes have always showed evidence of great technical skill. Drawing was not one of Versace's greatest strengths; he worked by creating rough sketches which he passed on to a subordinate designer to transcribe into something a pattern cutter could follow, and by pinning fabric on to a mannequin. Versace was consistently heralded for exploring daring contrasts of materials, with great originality. In the 1980s, for example, he appliquéd black leather with velvet and used grey flannel with shiny silk, while in the 1990s, black leather was embroidered with beads, and a clear vinyl yoke was set into an otherwise demure cream wool dress.

According to Richard Martin, in his biography, *Versace*, his skill with drapery was inspired by the work of the famous inter-war Paris haute couturiers, Madeleine Vionnet and Madame Grès; certainly, Versace owes much to these designers. Like most Italian designers of his generation, he knew about cut, which he learnt from his mother at an early age. Few questioned his understanding of tailoring; the clothes were cut to shape, support and flatter, with padding here, and a well-judged dart there, slimming waists, elongating legs and swelling breasts the world over. Anyone who has ever worn his designs will testify not only to the glamour of his designs but also to the way in which they hold and flatter the figure.

Versace's designs are well-suited to a model's shape, but the physique that is not quite so well-maintained also benefits, being reconstructing into a more ideal form and making Versace attractive to a much wider audience. As Susannah Barron wrote in *The Guardian* (16 July 1997): "a strappy Versace evening dress which curves around the body before flaring out

"VERSACE CLOTHES ARE QUITE hard to get into AND OUT OF. THE DRESSES ALL HAVE INNER BODICES THAT ZIP UP UNDERNEATH THE DRESS . . . [THAT'S] THE SECRET. THAT'S WHAT SQUEEZES YOU IN AND PUSHES YOU UP AND FLATTENS WHATEVER NEEDS FLATTENING . . . VERSACE MAKES ME FEEL LIKE A million dollars"

– LESLEY CLARKE, WIFE OF HAIRDRESSER TO THE STARS NICKY CLARKE, IN AN ARTICLE, "FOR LOVE OF VERSACE", IN *THE INDEPENDENT*, JULY, 1997.

into a flirtatious kick, slashed to the thigh and with the deepest neckline in the business, is quite the most sensual garment any woman could hope to wear". This is a not-insignificant point when assessing the reasons for Versace's success. In November 1999, Elizabeth Hurley described her first encounter with Versace in *Elle*:

"WITHIN MINUTES MY JEANS AND T-SHIRT WERE whipped off AND I WAS DRESS shoehorned INTO A GOLD SNAKESKIN NUMBER AND SIX-INCH "SLAVEGIRL" SANDALS. A BEVY OF EXQUISITELY UNIFORMED SEAMSTRESSES DESCENDED ON ME AND EMBARKED ON orgy of pinning and tucking ... I WAS USHERED, GIBBERING, INTO HAIR AND MAKE UP. AN HOUR LATER, MOUSY ENGLISH GIRL WAS TRANSFORMED INTO versace siren."

Two key facets encapsulate the essence of Versace's style: the overt display of wealth and sexuality. These determinants form the basis for the creation of the fantasy. Versace's early designs were casual and clean-cut, using materials in an experimental way, in precisely the mould created by Italian fashion pioneers in the 1950s and 1960s. However, the Versace label soon became famous for its blatantly sexy, body-revealing clothes, brash prints and the ostentatious use of gilt. The combination of sex, money and fashion guaranteed international press coverage and this, in turn, guaranteed sales.

Versace claimed that his love for erotic clothes stemmed from walks taken with his mother as a child in a staunchly Catholic community, when she attempted to shield his eyes as they passed the local brothel. He remembered the gaudy prostitutes as powerful, exotic and sensual beings.

Donatella, known as "the flash behind Gianni's dash", with her bottle-blonde hair, toned body and glitzy style, drew him further down the path of aggressive sexuality by encouraging him to make his clothes shorter, brighter, and above all, more raunchy. One of the better-known examples of this so-called "bordello chic" is the lingerie-lace and silk crêpe baby-doll mini-dresses, worn with Louis XIV-style heels, from 1991 to 1992.

Versace maintained his fashionability by tapping into the contemporary "zeitgeist", and it is hard to over-emphasize the significance of street-style in his work. "You know how many ideas I steal from the street?" he asked in *W* magazine in March 1992.

In the early 1980s, for example, he created his first metal mesh dress. It resembled, said a writer in *The Independent*,(16 July 1997), "mercury dripping imperceptibly slowly over a woman's curves" and threw more than a glance to London punks. This signature fabric remained a favourite theme throughout his career.

Versace's autumn/winter 1992–3 collection borrowed wholesale from the underworld of sado-masochism. Models wore bodice-harnesses and studded leather skirts with gladiator sandals. By this stage, neither press nor international jet-set could resist. As the 1990s progressed, the Versace look softened in line with the mood of fashion, but remained firmly rooted in the display of wealth and sexuality.

As with most designers, Versace's own cultural inheritance was a major inspiration in his work. He has frequently been described as "typically Italian", yet, in reality, he represents only one of the two major elements in Italian fashion's national stylistic identity. The first is the quiet, pared-down sophisticated look most commonly associated with Giorgio Armani and northern Italy. While some of Versace's lesser-known designs could slot neatly into this category, his signature looks were firmly entrenched in the more colourful, flamboyant glamour associated with the south.

Versace often explained how strongly influenced he was by southern Italian history. His personal libraries were reputedly brimming with over 10,000 volumes of art history and many of the images found their way into his work in stylized form – his ubiquitous Medusa's head is probably the best-known example.

However, he also grew up with idealized visions of both Italy and America, sold to the world through cinema in the 1950s and 1960s. Lured by cheap production costs, Hollywood went to Italy to make films; in the seductive world of "Hollywood on the Tiber", voluptuous Italian stars, such as Gina Lollobrigida and Sophia Loren, as well as a host of American stars, were portrayed as elegant, sexy, but above all, glamorous. This was a time when almost everyone went to the cinema frequently and Versace cannot have avoided its impact. It seems likely that cinematic images helped to inspire the creation of Versace's sirens several decades later.

Such an understanding of this important aspect of America's attitude to style may have furthered Versace's success in the USA. Versace was undoubtedly celebrated in America, nowhere more so than in Hollywood. In the mid-1990s, the Versace company targeted America, in a well-publicized attempt to make the USA its biggest export market. This included a planned flotation on the New York stock exchange.

Nonetheless, Versace's most important market, especially in his formative years, was in Italy itself. Although his designs did not appeal to the understated chic of many northern Italians, 24 per cent of Versace's market is still Italian, 5 per cent more than the North America market. His style appealed to the exuberant side of the Italian nature, and his vibrant use of colour reflected the Mediterranean climate, especially in the south. His core market was the so-called "Signora", the established woman who is perhaps not in the first flush of youth, but is keen to convey her sexuality and her wealth.

Versace was also enviably successful in most other countries, even in those not traditionally associated with his style. It may seem, for example, as if Versace's brand of sex and glamour would be the opposite of British "puritanism", the British fondness for dressing-down and simple clothing. Yet Versace tapped into a second important strain in British national stylistic identity: the new-money tendency to dress-up.

As Versace seemed instinctively to understand, in all countries there are people who delight in the display of sexuality and wealth. All he needed to do was to convince them that it was specifically his brand which could best convey such notions, and he used an impressive armoury of seductive weapons in his crusade.

The earliest weapon that Versace produced was the fashion model. Almost as soon as he set up his own label, Versace employed eminent American photographer Richard Avedon to shoot Brooke Shields, Janice Dickenson, Gia, Kim Alexis and Jerry Hall, the top models of the day, for a conspicuous advertising campaign.

By the mid-1980s, his catwalk shows were renowned for their theatrical excess, and became synonymous with loud music, bright lights and bare breasts, but above all, the "supermodel". Even when it was beyond his means, Versace would hire top models, not just one or two, but fifteen at a time, filling the runway with potential front-page pictures. He was said to be the first designer to offer models £10,000 per show, paying Christy Turlington a reputed £50,000 in return for exclusivity. Lush advertising campaigns continued to be created in collaboration with famous photographers like Bruce Weber and Helmut Newton.

Unlike Versace's womenswear, the menswear does not tend to make international headlines, and as such is not central to the group's success, although it has continued to represent a significant section of Versace profits.

In the 1990s, Versace published a series of expensive, glossy, coffee-table books, packed with supermodels and superstars, photographed, naturally, by big-name photographers. These books were central to the dissemination of the Versace dream.

The last book published before Versace's death was *Rock and Royalty*, at £57 a copy. It featured photographs of "royalty", such as the Duke of Windsor and Mrs Simpson, Napoleon and Diana, Princess of Wales alongside shots of the Versace family, various rock stars and models, and was intended as a light-hearted representation of varieties of human greatness. The book's charity launch party was to be attended by Diana but she withdrew her support at the last moment because, it was said, she did not wish to offend the British royal family. The book encapsulates Versace's vision, but can also be seen as an attempt to give his work meaning and permanence, as well as to bestow status upon himself and his family.

" I LIKE TO DRESS EGOS ", VERSACE FAMOUSLY SAID, NOT LEAST BECAUSE SUCH names EASILY persuade THE GENERAL PUBLIC THAT A VERSACE LABEL CAN AUTOMATICALLY CONVEY a sexually charged CELEBRITY UPON THEM.

Before *Rock and Royalty* came several other books, notably *Do Not Disturb*, a collection of Bruce Weber photographs of Versace's Italian homes in Italy and America, which conveyed Versace's vision of sumptuous opulence very, very, clearly. Versace lived like a star, but more importantly, in newspapers, magazines and in the book, he was seen to live like a star. The Versace lifestyle was presented through heavily stylized images, not only of his clothes, but also the lavish Versace house, the opulent Versace furniture, and the Versace product. Perhaps the most enduring images are Madonna in a white Versace bikini painting the toenails of a white poodle, and Claudia Schiffer and Sylvester Stallone wearing nothing except Versace plates over their genitals.

Cynics saw Versace's readiness to sponsor the arts as a clever exercise in ensuring his place in posterity. Certainly, it won him credibility, kudos, power and a sympathetic press.

Versace's extensive work for the theatre, opera and ballet and his links with the Metropolitan Museum of Art in New York are well-documented; there are several flattering books, exhibitions, any number of articles, and an impressive amount of web space. Following a Versace exhibition at the Victoria and Albert Museum in the mid-1980s, ex-Victorian and Albert Museum curator Sir Roy Strong is said to have declared his wish to be buried in his Versace trousers.

Versace's "flagship" stores in the world's capital cities were the perfect places to celebrate the Versace dream. In 1997, for example, a reported £11 million was spent turning an old bank on London's Bond Street into a Romanesque palace, with frescoed ceiling, 700 square metres of Sienese marble, a kilo of gold leaf, and shipments of antique furniture; even the toilets were made of marble. When Versace arrived in London to open his emporium, *The Guardian* newspaper reported (18 July 1997) that the crowds behind the police-barriers shouted "Gianni, Gianni", as he walked towards the gold-plated door, with "a galaxy of stars in tow".

Perhaps Versace's greatest talent of all was his gift for making very useful friends and claiming the obligations of friendship; he was undoubtedly the fashion world's most successful social networker. Described as "touchingly star-struck", Versace told *W* magazine in 1992: "It's my dream! Who can believe it? Sting called me this morning. I love it when rock or opera stars call and say, 'Gianni do this for me, or let's do this together'".

He played their music at his shows and in his shops and gave them clothes. Yet Versace was far too canny to be simply "star-struck". It was, of course, a mutually beneficial arrangement; he was well aware that he could secure invaluable publicity from associating with stars.

Consequently, the Versace client list comprises an impressive range of international stars from the worlds of film, television, and pop music: Cher, Kim Basinger, Joan Collins, Sylvester Stallone, Michael Jackson, Sting, Bruce Springsteen, Elton John, Madonna and, latterly, Patsy Kensit, All Saints, Posh Spice and David Beckham, Cate Blanchett, Anna Friel and Robbie Williams, to name but a few.

Without a doubt, few designers were better suited to the glitz of Hollywood than Versace. When performers had only a few seconds before the cameras at award ceremonies such as the Oscars, Versace made sure they were not ignored, and such appearances made sure that millions of ordinary people wanted to buy into the Versace dream.

Tremendous efforts were made to lend high-profile stars high- profile clothes for high-profile events, such as film premieres, even if this involved flying them to Milan for fitting. A flurry of faxes would then be sent to ensure that journalists knew in advance who would be wearing Versace at this ceremony or that.

"THAT DRESS", BARELY HELD TOGETHER WITH safety pins, LENT TO LIZ HURLEY AND WORN WHEN SHE ACCOMPANIED HER FAMOUS BOYFRIEND, HUGH GRANT, TO THE 1994 PREMIERE OF *FOUR WEDDINGS AND A FUNERAL*, HAS FREQUENTLY BEEN DESCRIBED AS VERSACE'S GREATEST COUP. LIZ HURLEY WAS CATAPULTED TO STARDOM OVERNIGHT. THE show-stopping power OF VERSACE WAS NEVER MORE APPARENT.

Show business personalities are not the only people with a high-profile. Versace was the first non-British designer label that Diana, Princess of Wales wore, and it is significant that when she emerged from her marriage debacle, she chose Versace to signal her more confident approach. For her iconoclastic *Vanity Fair* cover in July 1997, she wore a white, one-shouldered Versace gown.

Versace was also more than happy to loan gowns to lesser celebrities, such as Tara Palmer-Tomkinson, who could give him his money back in press coverage. When a colour page advertisement in British *Vogue* costs over £14,000, plus the model's and photographer's fees, it is not difficult to understand why he did it. Versace was not alone in utilizing such arrangements, nor was he the first, but he was certainly a master of it, and "courted" stars tirelessly in order to exploit its full potential.

Nonetheless, these arrangements were not meant to replace the more traditional promotional methods, rather to reinforce them. Versace continued to spend a small fortune on magazine advertising, taking twenty pages in *Vogue*, when other top designers might have four or five. This gave him considerable leverage with the editorial departments of such glossy magazines.

Versace understood the value of different forms of self-promotion, perhaps more than any other fashion designer, and he was acutely aware that his high-fashion clothes represented only a small part of his turnover. The more pictures he produced of his "perfect" family, enjoying "perfect" holidays, surrounded by luxury and superstar friends, the more he developed his mythical status; the more, too, he developed the value of the Versace name and the more the ordinary consumer wanted to buy into his world. As British fashion designer Alexander McQueen told *The Independent* (18 September 1999), "Any interest in the clothes is secondary to interest in a designer".

The success of the Milanese fashion industry, of which Versace was a part, was based precisely on an understanding that high fashion no longer made its profits from the creation of exquisite made-to-measure clothes for a very rich clientele. Versace introduced his "atelier" line in 1993; such haute couture collections, presented in extravagant fashion shows bursting with celebrities, rarely make money. The number of people in the world who will pay £10,000 for a dress has dwindled to around 3,000.

However, as all fashion designers know, there are millions of people who can afford to pay £30 for a designer perfume or £15 for a lipstick. Versace cosmetics account for 12 per cent of company turnover, while accessories represent an impressive 21 per cent. But for people to part with their money, they must be convinced that they are getting more than just a bottle of scent; they must be seduced by a dream, and haute couture was a key facet of the Versace fantasy.

As well as the devotees of Versace's lipsticks and scents, there is an important group of wealthy "middle-class" consumers who could afford both the clothes and the lifestyle products. Although this level of consumption is naturally much harder to pinpoint, because it is not generally publicized, a number of well-heeled women have explained to the press why they wear Versace. Lesley Clarke described in *The Independent* (7 July 1997), "what wearing Versace does for her". She told how she wore her first Versace dress to 10 Downing Street: "It was daring and mint green, and didn't leave anything to the imagination. It stood out among the grey suits. John Major looked a bit gobsmacked . . . they were all wearing twinsets and pearls, and everyone just stared at me." This was obviously the desired effect: "Since then", Mrs Clarke went on, "I have bought about half a dozen atelier [haute couture] dresses", describing them as "drop-dead glamorous ... result dresses".

Lesley Clarke also addressed the issue of Versace and female empowerment: "I've seen lots of women wearing Versace who look glamorous but don't necessarily look powerful – rich men's wives." These are people for whom appearance, in terms of maintaining a high-profile public image, is paramount. Several "wives of rich men" whose "husbands had turned them on to [Versace's] sensual style" were featured in *You* magazine back in May 1995, under the heading "The World's Most Glamorous Fan Club". In the article, Clarke commented that "I think that there's a bit of a contradiction between the way Nicky sees me and the way I think of myself. He sees me as a vamp, I think ... my own instincts veer towards Armani ... ". Suzy Barnes, wife of footballer John Barnes, explained: "It's result-wear; people always comment. I buy everything: leisurewear, dressing gowns, towels". Tonia Hall, wife of a wealthy businessman, said simply: "My husband enjoys glamour".

Glamour is a word that arises repeatedly when the work of Gianni Versace is analyzed, but it seems that it is a certain type of glamour, one that is clearly defined in the minds of men who enjoy their partners wearing Versace, one that can be intrinsically linked to the creation of sexual fantasy. There has been considerable debate about whether Versace's clothes empower or subjugate women, and it is significant that the *You* article suggests that a high proportion of the women who habitually wear Versace were "introduced to the label" by what is described as "a style-conscious partner".

In *The Fashion Conspiracy* (1988), fashion editor Nick Coleridge describes a revealing encounter with a woman wearing Versace, which is pertinent here. Coleridge observed an encounter with a couple in a Milanese restaurant, a 70-year-old man accompanied by a 40-year-old blonde woman who was wearing "a dress made entirely of black leather: black leather shoulders, black leather bodice, tight black leather skirt ... It exuded a raunchy glamour quite different from anything I had seen." Coleridge quotes the older man who told him: "I chose all Luisa's clothes. After all, it is I who have to look at them ... Gianni Versace is the best designer. He makes dresses which make women look like women". Whether men or women, however, all these people seemed happy to either be sold or wear a piece of Versace's glamour, to able to join in his success.

Despite its success, the Versace family was not without its problems. By the mid-1990s, there were increasing rumours about tempestuous rows between Donatella and Gianni himself and considerable press attention was devoted to Versace's finances. Then, in the winter and spring of 1996, it was revealed that Versace had suffered a rare cancer of the inner ear, which was said to have been cured by surgery and chemotherapy. In response, the promotional balance of the company changed from "Gianni Versace" to '"Versace"; there was a marked fall in the amount of press interviews with Versace and a rise in the number of interviews with Donatella.

Gianni Versace was shot dead outside his Miami villa on 15 July 1997, by the serial killer Andrew Cunanan. The dramatic murder made headlines round the world. There were obituaries aplenty, most of them flattering, and many people were clearly saddened by his death. Diana, Princess of Wales, for one, said she was "devastated". In the weeks that followed there was an unseemly fight to publish books about his life and make films about his death, and within seven months the "Secret Lives" documentary was screened on British television.

In 1996, the year before Versace's death, the group is said to have made a profit of over £25 million on a turnover of £569 million. Versace himself was reputedly insured with Lloyds of London for £25 million, under its "key man" policy. Versace left the bulk of his fortune to his 11-year old niece Allegra, and his collection of paintings, reputed to be worth £40 million, to his 8-year old nephew Daniel.

Control of the fashion house rested with Santo and Donatella, 40-year-old Donatella assuming all design responsibilities and 53-year old Santo continuing as the group's chief executive. Versace's companion, Antonio d'Amico, was reported to have received £20,000 a month, for life. Not surprisingly, the proposed flotation of Versace shares was postponed indefinitely.

It was always likely that the label would survive his death. As Donatella herself told the fashion trade's bible *Women's Wear Daily* in July 1998, "Gianni left us such a healthy company. I'm doing what I can to keep that going. But if I wasn't here, it's not as if the house would close. We would have just hired another designer, and that would have been that".

It was by no means certain that Donatella herself would make the grade. Certainly, her first two collections met with mixed reactions, but the company has since flourished, and her clothes are rarely off the front pages. The ready-to-wear collections seemed to come easily – not surprising, since she had plenty of experience in that sphere. The biggest challenge was the "atelier" haute couture collection which was crucial to the reinforcement of the Versace fantasy. At first, it seemed as though Donatella would adhere closely to the tried and tested Versace formula. As she told *W* magazine in November 1997,

"I GREW UP WITH GIANNI AND I STARTED WORK WITH Versace, SO I'M NOT GOING TO HAVE ANOTHER philosophy."

By time the first collection was shown in July 1998, it was clear that she had grown in confidence, and rather than attempting to reproduce her brother's style, as she had with her other collections, here she wanted to develop her own. As she told *Women's Wear Daily* (16 July 1998): "It's important to make one thing very clear up front ... I need to find my own formula for couture."

Although Versace had pared-down his style for the last collection before his death, in line with the mood of contemporary fashion, the look that Donatella created for the couture catwalk was distinctly quieter and more modern than her brother's. The silhouette remained figure-hugging, the impact remained sexy, telling *WWD*, "it's not trashy or loud, which Versace can be sometimes ... this is much more strict and severe, with a bit of irreverence." She pinpointed a full-length red horsehair, silk, cotton and spandex dress with mink seams. Nonetheless, the intention remained to "really make a statement ... something that will get you noticed".

The promotion of Versace is also changing. The spring/summer 1999 advertising campaign for Versace couture, seen in Italian *Vogue* and *W*, caused something of a sensation. Instead of using the supermodels, such as Naomi Campbell, that the Versace label had been so famously associated with, she and photographer Steven Meisel brought in new models, including Frankie Ryder and fast-rising star Devon Aoki.

The campaign reinforced the conscious move away from Gianni Versace's approach, away from the brash, sexually charged campaigns of old. As Donatella told *The Times* in April 1999, "This is about updating the image of the company." Versace describes the new approach rather obliquely as "modernity", explaining the marketing by saying that "the clothes were so modern, so we used a traditional approach to highlight the modernity" (*The Times*, 3 April 1999). The styling, with its belle époque opulence, stuffed birds and swathes of rich fabric appears to be informed by the work of John Galliano, a fashion designer often termed "post-modern".

The autumn/winter 1999 collection was promoted with a neo-Gothic post-party look, with eerily pale faces, sunken eyes, frizzy unkempt hair, all alluding to a drug-induced haze. As Professor Ian Griffiths, Head of Fashion at Kingston University in London and consultant designer at MaxMara, explains, "when Gianni Versace made his name, overt sexuality was shocking; today, that same sexuality would seem too mainstream to be exciting." Contemporary cutting-edge fashion is governed by a less healthy-looking, even "'wasted" look, which has come directly from street-style. Although the look has changed, Donatella

Versace is tapping into the zeitgeist, just as, in his prime, her brother did so successfully.

The look may be changing, but the company continues to exploit the high-fashion fantasy image. In terms of maintaining the show business side of Versace's PR operations, Donatella has always worked extremely hard at developing good relations with stars, especially rock and pop stars, and, true to Versace form, described Madonna as her "favourite person in the world" in May 1999, according to The Independent. At the 1999 Oscars, Versace maintained its high profile, with their designs being worn by Madonna and Catherine Zeta Jones, among others.

The latest Versace venture is a chain of "lifestyle" hotels, or "Palazzi Versace", the first of which, on the Australian Gold Coast, is due to open in September 2000 at a cost of $250 million. According to the Versace company, four of the rooms will be "the largest in the world" and "everything will be over-the-top", with huge beds, and huge jacuzzis, in unmistakable Versace style.

Gianni Versace was not a "God of fashion", nor a "genius", as some would have us believe. He was neither reactionary, nor revolutionary. He was a talented designer and a remarkably aslute business-man, with a gift for capturing the mood, injecting it with a shot of sex and glamour, promoting it and selling it, not only to the stars he was photographed with, but more significantly, to the millions of ordinary people who enjoyed the Versace fantasy. His sister spent long enough working alongside him to understand this and has taken up his mantle with aplomb. Moreover, she seems to be infusing the Versace label with a new vigour which will take it into the third millennium.

"THERE ARE MANY more PEOPLE WHO CAN SPEND LESS MONEY than PEOPLE WHO CAN SPEND A LOT OF MONEY ... THAT'S WHERE THE FUTURE IS."

DONATELLA VERSACE,
W MAGAZINE, NOVEMBER 1997.

BAROQUE

Signature baroque pattern on Versace porcelain
– photograph by Bruce Weber.

GIANNI VERSACE

The designer takes the applause
of the supermodels on the catwalk, 1993.

GIANNI VERSACE/HELENA CHRISTENSEN

Left: Versace at home with his art treasures.
Right: Helena Christensen wears exotic printed Versace
"Miami" silk scarves, 1993.

EVENING GOWN

Body-hugging fuschia evening gown with
slit-to-hip skirt and gold safety pin detail, 1994.

GIANNI AND DONATELLA/MADONNA

Left: Gianni and sister Donatella, 1995.
Right: Madonna wears a typically spectacular
Versace gown at the Brit Awards, 1998.

BROOKE SHIELDS/JERRY HALL

Brooke Shields (left) and Jerry Hall
(right, in metal mesh), both photographed
by Richard Avedon, for Versace in the early 1980s.

SKETCHES

Designs for daywear, 1988,
left and evening wear 1990, (right).

ROYALTY AND ROCK

Donatella talks to Prince Charles (left)
and poses with Madonna and Elton John (right).

STING AND TRUDIE/DIANA

Sting and Trudie Styler are married in Versace (left).
Diana, Princess of Wales wearing a simple, striking purple
evening gown with a matching Versace purse.

ELIZABETH HURLEY/CATHERINE ZETA JONES

Elizabeth Hurley (left) reveals her leopard-print Versace
knickers at the wedding of friends.
Catherine Zeta Jones (right) wears a dramatic strapless scarlet
gown by Versace to the 1999 Academy Awards.

POP ART

Linda Evangelista models a pop-art inspired evening dress and accessories, 1990 (left). A heavily beaded jumpsuit (right) that draws attention to the embossed representation of Marilyn Monroe's lips.

CHRISTY TURLINGTON

Christy Turlington wears the total Versace look (left), 1991 and (right) models a beaded jumpsuit inspired by *Vogue*.

BAROQUE

Left: Helena Christensen wear's Versace's opulent gold baroque print, photographed by Herb Ritts, 1991. Versace silk scarf in "wild baroque print (right), 1990.

COLOUR AND GRAPHICS

Versace combined rock graphics with typically bold colour (left), 1991. A melting pot of patterns, colours and the Versace logo combine in a 1991 outfit (right) that cannot be ignored.

HELENA CHRISTENSEN

Helena Christensen wears jewellery as clothing, (left) 1992. Modelling the "Miami" collection, (right) 1993.

"SAFETY-PIN"

Fuchsia safety pin dress, (left) 1994 and Elizabeth Hurley wears a coy expression in "that dress" at the UK premiere of *Four Weddings and a Funeral*, with partner Hugh Grant.

EVENING WEAR

Sensational "barely there" evening dress (left), encrusted with drop crystals, 1995. Gilt-buckled leather-banded evening dress, (right) 1992, which casts more than a glance at sadomasochism.

METAL

Linda Evangelista wears one of Versace's sensual and fluid metallic dresses, (left) 1995. A trio of supermodels parade in metal mesh (right), 1994.

PLASTIC

Christy Turlington (left) wears a black plastic tank dress, 1994. Elton John (right), in an emerald plastic suit, poses with models, photographed by Richard Avedon 1993.

CORSETRY/WEDDING DRESS

Externalized corsetry, (left) 1995. The Versace bride (right) wears silver metal mesh, 1995.

DAYWEAR/SWIMWEAR

Kate Moss (left) models Versace's colourful,
yet wearable daywear, 1995.
Eyecatching semi-transparent swimwear
a heart motif (right), 1997.

SUITING/SIMPLE STYLE

Naomi Campbell (left) struts in signature
Versace sharp suit, with micro-skirt, 1997.
Karen Elson (right) models a simpler
Versace look for evening, 1997.

EASY

Easy-to-wear (left) Versace,
Autumn 1999. Sensual leather jacket (right)
photographed by Richard Avedon, 1997.

DONATELLA'S DESIGNS

Body-hugging simplicity (left), and
colour contrast with modern lines (right)
both by Donatella Versace, 1998.

DONATELLA

Hand-in-hand with Kate Moss and Naomi Campbell, Donatella
takes her applause on the catwalk, 1998.

KATE AND NAOMI

Kate Moss (left) carries a white leather
Versace bag, emblazoned with the Medusa logo, 1995.
Naomi Campbell (right) in a spectacular
cutaway "cobweb" dress by Donatella Versace, 1998.

ATELIER VERSACE

The spring 1999 Versace couture
collection, photographed by Steve Meisel.

1999

Rauchy rock-chic from Donatella (left), 1999.
Her delicate Neo-Gothick look for 1999 (right).

1999

Versace for the end of the millennium (left), male
rock-star style. Kate Moss (right) wears
Donatella's light and airy diamanté evening gown.

Picture credits

The publishers would like to thank the following sources for their kind permission to reproduce the pictures in this book:

All Action 8, 9, 32, 55, 62

PA News 2/3, 33, 34, 35, 58, 63, 67, 68, 72

Famous/Fred Duval 47

Niall McInerney 5, 7, 39, 42, 43, 44, 45, 46, 48, 49, 50, 51, 52, 54, 64/65, 66

Retna/Bill Davila 56/Robert Fairer 57

Rex Features 60

Gianni Versace/Richard Avedon Autumn/Winter 1980-81 26

Gianni Versace/Richard Avedon Spring/Summer 1983 27

Gianni Versace/Richard Avedon Spring/Summer 1995 Elton John, Nadja Auermann and Kristen McMenamy 53

Gianni Versace/Richard Avedon Autumn/Winter 1997–1998 with Kristen McMenamy (model) 61

Gianni Versace/Richard Avedon Autumn/Winter 1997-1998 59

Gianni Versace/Massimo Listri 4

Atelier Versace/Steven Meisel Autumn/Winter 1999-2000 68/69

Gianni Versace/Irving Penn Spring/Summer 1992 36

Gianni Versace/Irving Penn Spring/Summer 1991 38

Gianni Versace/Herb Ritts Autumn/Winter 1991–1992 40

Atelier Versace/Tyen Autumn/Winter 1991-1992 37

Gianni Versace/Bruce Weber Spring Summer 1995 1

Gianni Versace/Werner 28, 29

Gianni Versace Spring/Summer 1992 41

Versace /June 1999 Diamonds Are Forever 30

Versace /Retrospective of Gianni Versace at Metropolitan Museum of Art, New York 1997 31

Gianni Versace Autumn/Winter 1999-2000 70, 71

Every effort has been made to acknowledge correctly and contact the source and/copyright holder of each picture, and Carlton Books Limited apologises for any unintentional errors or omissions which will be corrected in future editions of this book.